SCHOLASTIC
News
Nonfiction Readers

Sally Ride

by
Catherine Nichols

Children's Press®
A Division of Scholastic Inc.
New York Toronto London Auckland Sydney
Mexico City New Delhi Hong Kong
Danbury, Connecticut

These content vocabulary word builders
are for grades 1-2.

Consultant: Dr. Jack Farmer
Astrobiology Investigator
Department of Geological Sciences, Arizona State University

Photo Credits:

All Photographs © 2005 NASA except: AP/Wide World Photos/Denis Poroy: 1, 19; Corbis Images: back cover, 4 bottom right, 7, 15 (Bettmann), 21 bottom, 23 top left, 23 bottom left (Roger Ressmeyer/NASA); Getty Images/NASA/AFP Photo: 4 bottom left, 10; PhotoDisc via SODA: 5 top left, 6, 17.

Book Design: Simonsays Design!

Library of Congress Cataloging-in-Publication Data

Nichols, Catherine.
    Sally Ride / by Catherine Nichols.
        p. cm. — (Scholastic news nonfiction readers)
    Includes bibliographical references and index.
    ISBN 0-516-24942-8 (lib. bdg.)   0-516-24785-9 (pbk.)
    1. Ride, Sally—Juvenile literature. 2. Women astronauts—United
        States—Biography—Juvenile literature. 3. Astronauts—United
        States—Biography—Juvenile literature. I. Title. II. Series.
    TL789.85.R53N53 2005
    629.45'0092—dc22

                                                         2005002105

1 2 3 4 5 6 7 8 9 10 R 14 13 12 11 10 09 08 07 06 05

CONTENTS

WORD HUNT

Look for these words as you read. They will be in **bold**.

astronauts
(**as**-truh-nawts)

NASA
(**nah**-suh)

Sally Ride
(**sal**-ee ride)

4

Earth
(urth)

float
(floht)

satellite
(**sat**-uh-lite)

space shuttle
(**spayss** shuht-uhl)

Meet Sally Ride

Only a few people have seen **Earth** from space.

Sally Ride is one of them.

Earth

Sally Ride is in a space shuttle. She is talking to people on the ground.

Sally liked to learn about the stars.

She studied them on Earth.

She didn't know that one day she would see the stars from space!

Sally is training to go into space.

NASA needed **astronauts**.

Astronauts are people who travel to space.

Sally tried out for the job.

NASA picked Sally to be one of the astronauts.

NASA in Florida

Sally

In 1983, Sally flew around Earth in a **space shuttle**.

She was the first American woman to do this.

Sally stayed in space for six days.

Sally inside space shuttle

This is the space
shuttle Sally flew in.

13

One of Sally's jobs in space was to test a robotic arm.

She had to make a robotic arm put a **satellite** in space.

A satellite is an object that humans use to find out about space.

satellite

Sally tested the robotic arm. It worked!

There is a lot of work to do in a space shuttle. But it is fun, too.

You **float** in outer space. You get to look at the Earth from above!

Aren't astronauts lucky?

Look! This is how Earth looks from space. Did Sally take any pictures?

Sally left NASA in 1987 to be a teacher.

She has not forgotten what it was like to be an astronaut.

It was hard work.

It was fun!

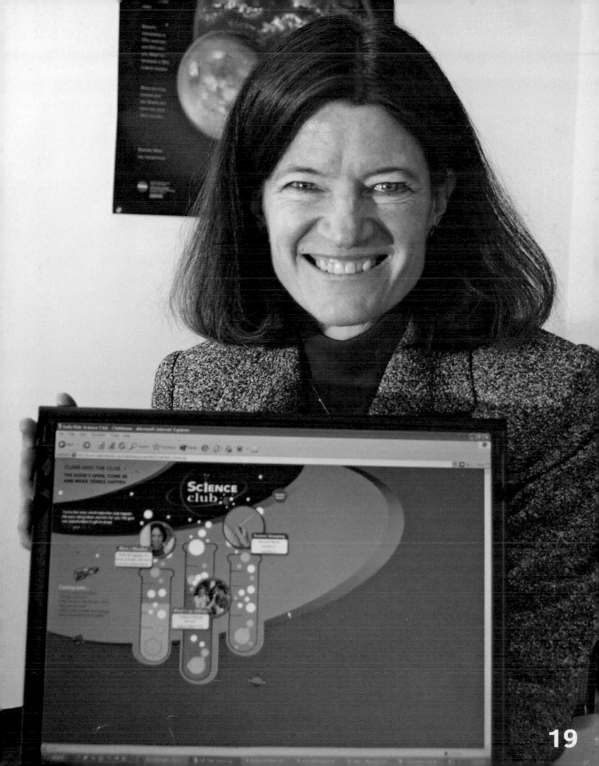

What's Up in Space?

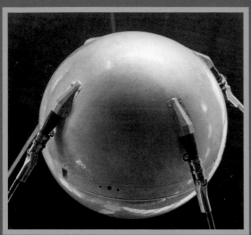

On October 4, 1957, *Sputnik 1* becomes the first satellite in space.

On July 20, 1969, Neil Armstrong becomes the first person on the Moon.

On June 18, 1983, Sally Ride becomes the first American woman to fly in space.

On September 12, 1992, Mae Jemison becomes the first African-American woman to fly in space.

5

4

On April 24, 1990, the Hubble Space Telescope is put into space. It takes many pictures of space.

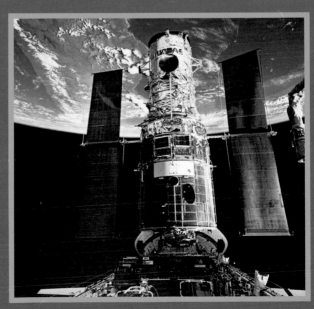

YOUR NEW WORDS

astronauts (**as**-truh-nawts)
people trained to travel in space

Earth (urth) the third planet from the Sun,
where we live

float (floht) to rest on water or air

NASA (**nah**-suh) the space program for
the United States of America

Sally Ride (**sal**-ee ride) the first American
woman to fly in space

satellite (**sat**-uh-lite) an object that
humans put into space to collect
information about space

space shuttle (**spayss** shuht-uhl)
a vehicle that astronauts use to fly into
space and study space

WHAT OTHER THINGS ARE USED IN SPACE?

The Hubble Space Telescope!

A lunar rover!

Solar panels!

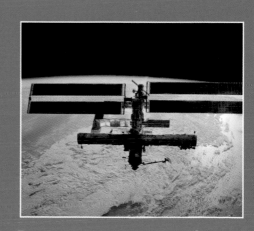

A space station!

INDEX

FIND OUT MORE

Book:

Sally Ride: Astronaut, Scientist by Pamela Hill Nettleton and Gary Nichols (Picture Windows Books, 2003)

Website: Dr. Sally Ride
http://starchild.gsfc.nasa.gov/docs/StarChild/whos_who_level2/ride.html

MEET THE AUTHOR:

Catherine Nichols is the author of many books for young readers. She especially likes to write biographies. Catherine has a country house in upstate New York. On clear nights, she likes to go outside and look at the stars.